In My Mother's Womb

In My Mother's Womb

Fr. Bill Deschamps, Christine Schroeder, Mary Roma, and Susan J. Bellavance

Illustrated by Dan Andreasen

Our Sunday Visitor
Huntington, Indiana

Our Sunday Visitor Publishing Division
Our Sunday Visitor, Inc.
200 Noll Plaza
Huntington, IN 46750
1-800-348-2440

ISBN: 978-1-68192-971-2 (Inventory No. T2699)
1. RELIGION—Christian Living—Family & Relationships.
2. RELIGION—Christian Living—Social Issues.
3. RELIGION—Christianity—Catholic.

eISBN: 978-1-68192-972-9
LCCN: 2023934673

Cover design: Tyler Ottinger
Interior design: Amanda Falk
Cover and interior art: Dan Andreasen

PRINTED IN THE UNITED STATES OF AMERICA

To the Mother of Jesus

We also warmly dedicate this book to those whose babies did not reach full term.

We offer this hope of faith — that every child has an eternal soul and will be restored to us in eternity, where every tear will be wiped away, every love restored, and all that was lost will be found in God.

INTRODUCTION

By Fr. Bill Deschamps

As a pastor, I hope to remind those in my care that Divine Love created each one of us with gifts and abilities, talents and personalities as unique as our own DNA. This awareness and conviction of our uniqueness, giftedness, and "chosenness" by God invariably leads to an awareness that life itself is God's greatest gift — a gift to be cherished, protected, and celebrated. To that end, our pro-life prayer team offers *In My Mother's Womb*, a story created to express the dynamic unfolding of life in the hopes that it will convey this message of uniqueness and love to the heart of every reader.

In diary form, this book is written from the perspective of the little soul, who engages the reader with enthralling wonder at the mysterious unfolding of his tiny, intricate body, vibrantly growing week by week. The little soul delightfully conveys the truth that every child conceived is a gift from God. The conception of the little soul occurs near the feast of the Holy Guardian Angels (October 2). This serves as a reminder that a guardian angel is given to each child from the very first moment of life. We finish forty weeks later by celebrating the birthday of the baby around Father's Day in June.

In sharing this work week by week from the pulpit, I have witnessed firsthand the joy of my parishioners at watching this life unfold. With accompanying Scripture verses each week this book becomes a fresh encounter with life and the Author of Life. It also provides an invitation to generosity, helping mothers in need through parish donations to the pregnancy outreach programs in our area. I hope that this work will spread far beyond the borders of our tiny New Hampshire town of Jaffrey.

WEEK 1

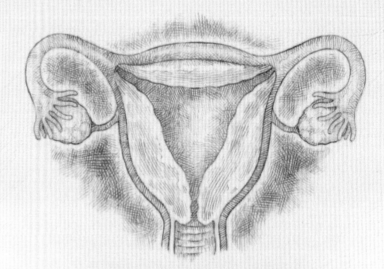

Before I formed you in the womb I knew you,
and before you were born I consecrated you.

— *Jeremiah 1:5*

God knows me! Though I am still a secret in his heart, God has called me by name from all eternity. Get ready, Mom and Dad; I am coming to you soon! During this first week, God is beginning to make hidden preparations for me. How wonderful to know I have always been loved, even before I came into the world!

WEEK 2

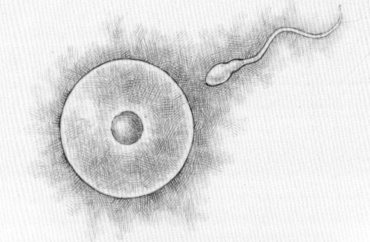

You know me right well;
  my frame was not hidden from you, when I
was being made in secret,
  intricately wrought in the
depths of the earth.

— Psalm 139:14–15

There is a warm and wonderful place being prepared for me inside my mom. I call it Mom's "baby pocket." Soon a bit of Mom and a bit of Dad will join together to form a brand new me! In that instant my soul comes to be, and *flash,* my little life twinkles like a star before the only eyes that can see me: God's!

WEEK 3

For he will give his angels charge of you
to guard you in all your ways.

— *Psalm 91:11*

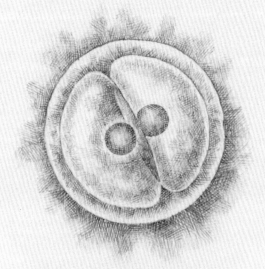

Glory, alleluia! I am smaller than a mustard seed, but everything that makes me a person is already here. Today is October 2, the feast of the guardian angels, and my guardian angel is right here with me. How God loves me!

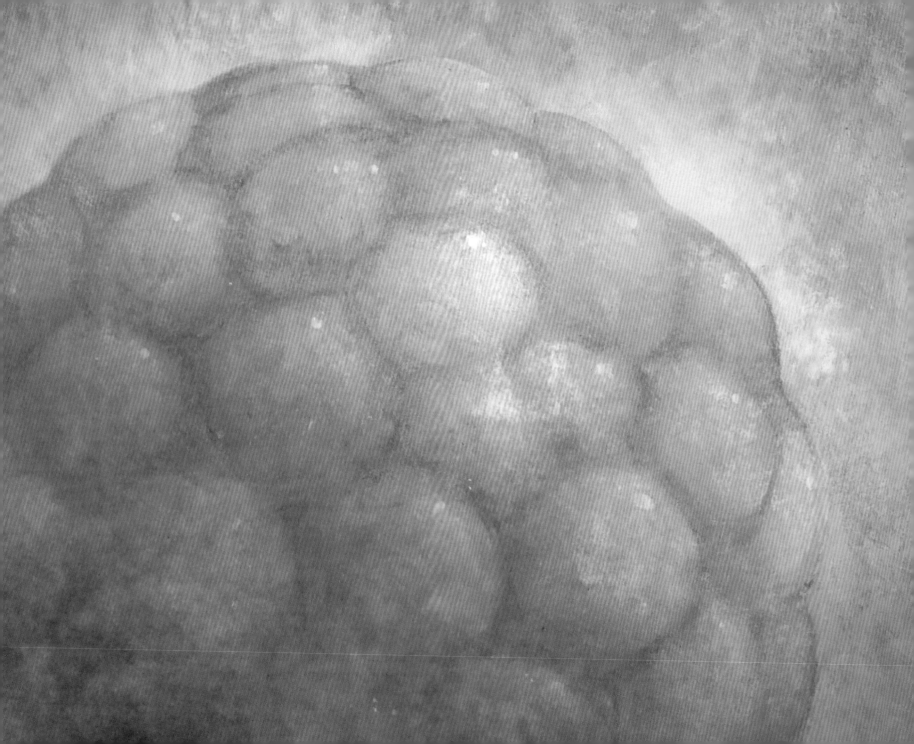

WEEK 4

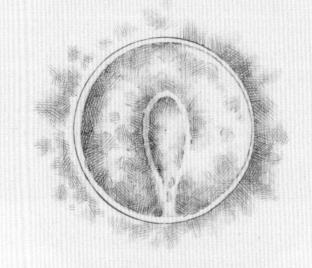

"Sacrifices and offerings you have not desired,
but a body have you prepared for me;
in burnt offerings and sin offerings you have taken no pleasure.
Then I said, 'Behold, I have come to do your will, O God,'
as it is written of me in the roll of the book."

— Hebrews 10:5–7

Although I am less than one-hundredth of an inch long, my cells are already forming into three different layers that will become my own unique body. I am protected and nourished in my special nesting place that will be my home for the next nine months. Mom and Dad will find out about me soon!

WEEK 5

For you formed my inward parts,
*   you knitted me together in my mother's*
*   womb.*
I praise you, for I am wondrously made.
*   Wonderful are your works!*

— Psalm 139:13–14

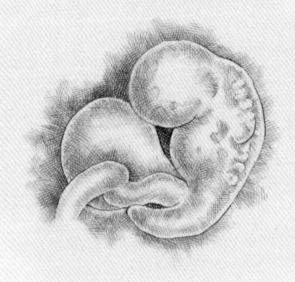

Even though I am just about the size of this comma, my very tiny heart started beating for the first time today. How can some people say that I am just a clump of cells? God's master plan is at work right here! He says that I am fearfully and wonderfully made.

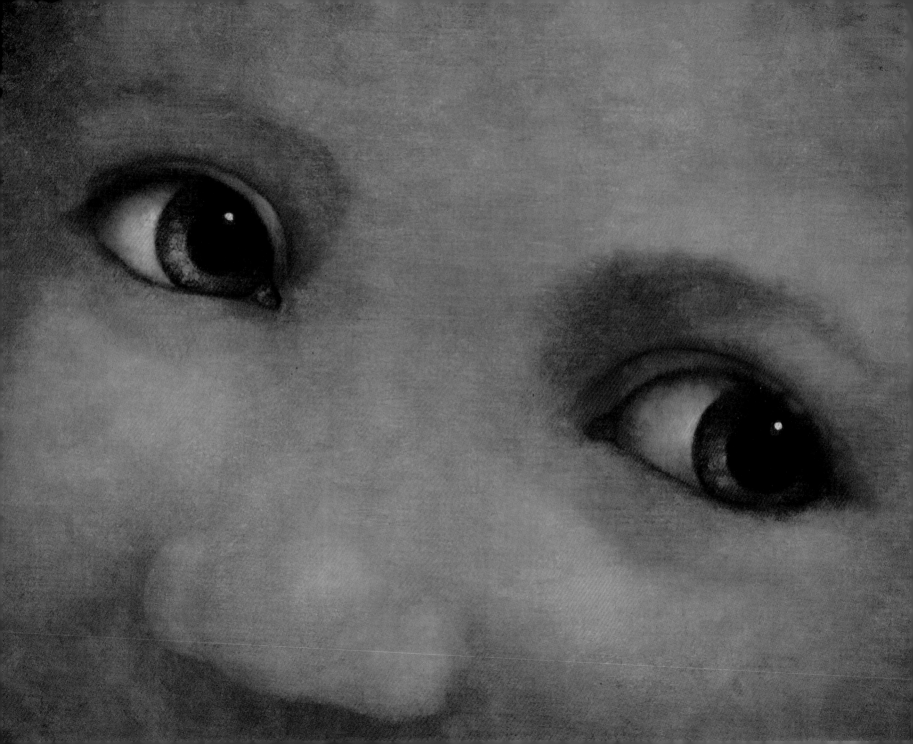

WEEK 6

Yet, O Lᴏʀᴅ, you are our Father;
  we are the clay, and you are our potter;
  we are all the work of your hand.

— Isaiah 64:8

My parents do not even know yet that I am here, but God knows the secret. He knows everything about me: whether I am a boy or a girl, the color of my eyes, hair, skin, and everything else. Just like the tiniest morsel of bread is still bread, this miniature version of me is still me.

WEEK 7

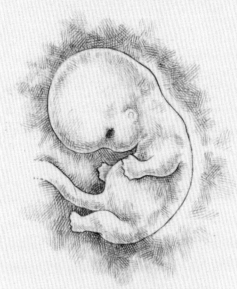

Having gifts that differ according to the grace given to us, let us use them.

— Romans 12:6

God knows other secrets about me: My arm and leg buds are starting to form, and all that makes me unique is already imprinted in my cells. Maybe I will like to draw, play sports, read books, sing, or dance. Who knows what other talents and interests I may have! But these traits are all part of me already.

WEEK 8

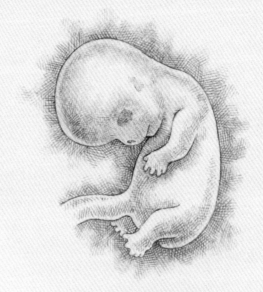

Then the LORD God formed man of dust from the ground, and breathed into his nostrils the breath of life; and man became a living soul.

— Genesis 2:7

If you could see me now, you'd think that I look a little more like a newborn baby, although I am about the size of a kidney bean. You would see the early stages of my nostrils, ears, and eyes, as well as my fingers and toes. And just think, I already have my sense of smell!

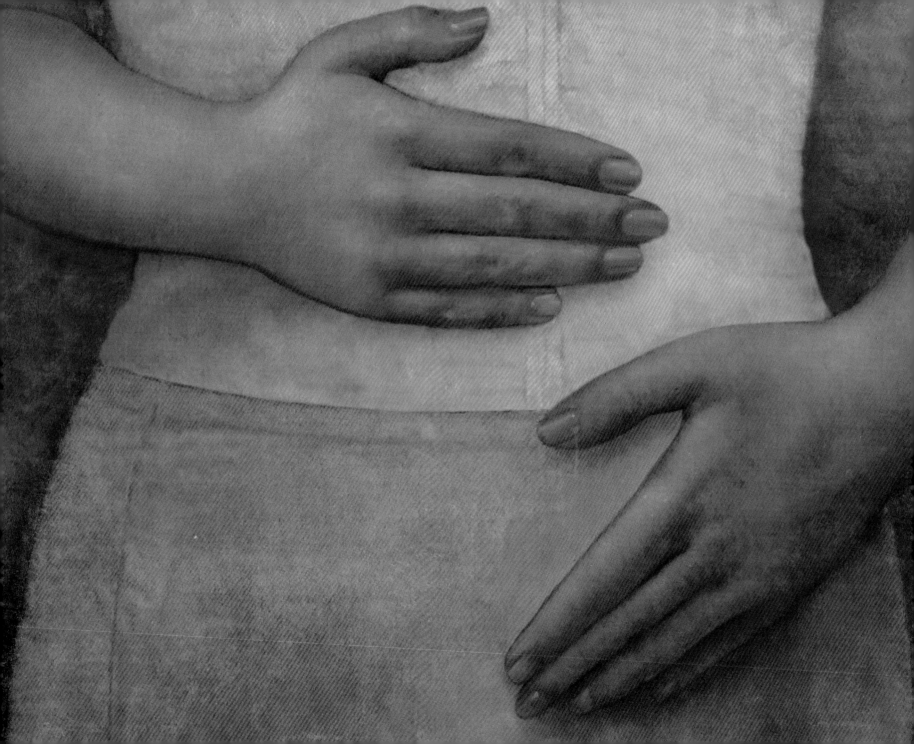

WEEK 9

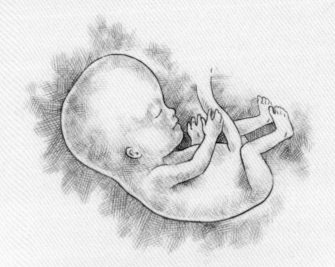

Whoever receives one such child
in my name receives me.

— *Matthew 18:5*

I've got elbows! You should see me practice bending and flexing them. I also have a sense of balance thanks to my inner ear, which is already being formed. It's never too early to begin my daily exercise routine — though I'm only about an inch long. Mom would be surprised to know all the things I can do. She hasn't even felt me yet!

WEEK 10

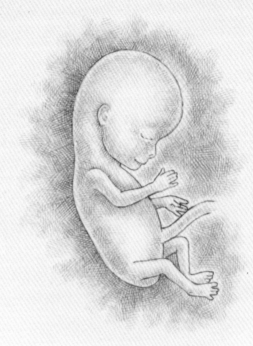

When I look at your heavens, the work of
*   your fingers,*
* the moon and the stars which you have*
*   established;*
what is man that you are mindful of him,
* and the son of man that you care for him?*

— Psalm 8:3–4

It's almost Thanksgiving, and my tongue is formed now and ready to taste my first turkey — well, maybe not just yet. I am about the size of a small plum, but I am growing by leaps and bounds! I am more than one fifth of the way on my journey toward being born. All my muscles, organs, and systems are formed. God's hand is connecting them so they will all work together as one united and amazing body.

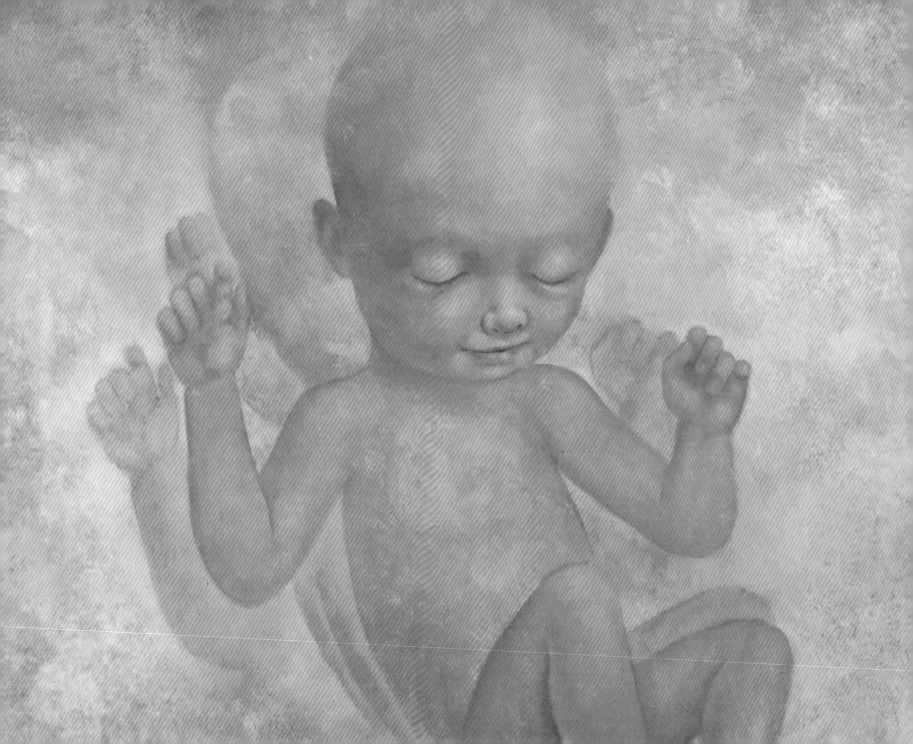

WEEK 11

Let them praise his name with dancing,
*   making melody to him*
with timbrel and lyre!

— Psalm 149:3

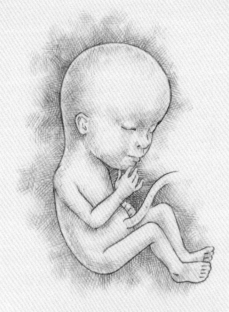

God and I have more secrets. My fingers are separated now. Some day soon, I will even have my own unique fingerprints. My toes are no longer webbed, which makes it easier to practice my new steps. Bet you didn't know I can dance! Well, I can't dance like you do yet, but I am wiggling, rolling, shifting around, and stretching, so it's my kind of dance. I call it the "Womba."

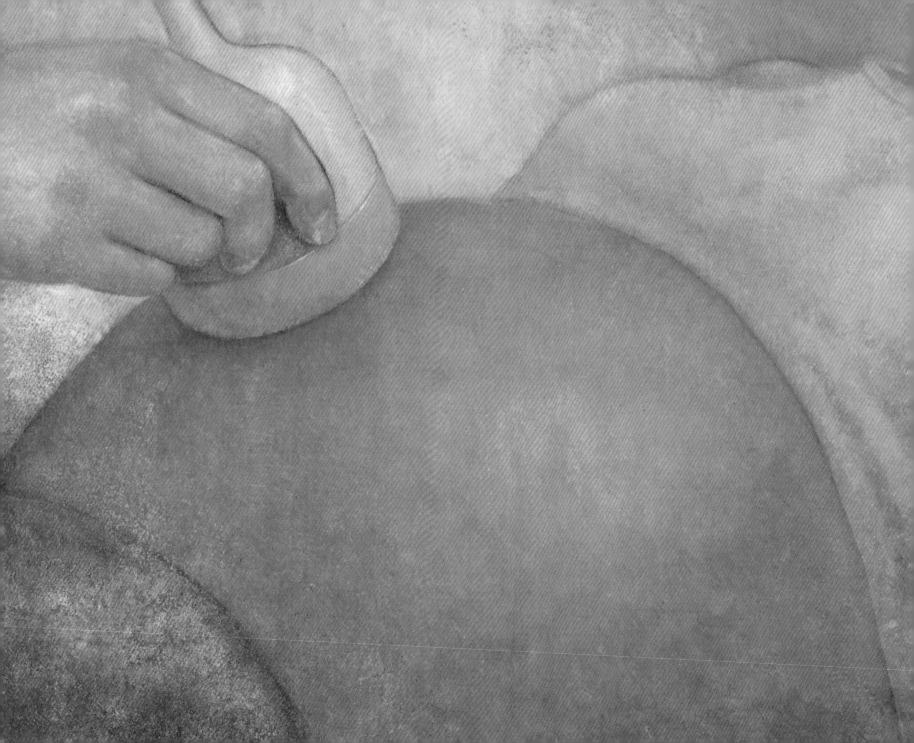

WEEK 12

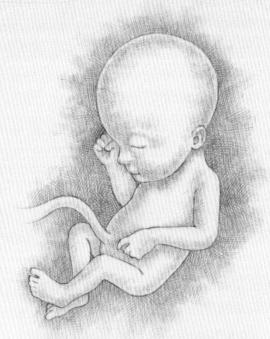

Create in me a clean heart, O God,
and put a new and right spirit within me.

— *Psalm 51:10*

Guess what — I am just over two inches long now. My tooth buds are appearing; my bones are getting stronger; my fingernails and toenails are growing; and I can even put my thumb in my mouth. But the most exciting part of all is that, with the help of the doctor's special instrument, Mom and Dad heard my heartbeat for the first time this week. It's a miracle!

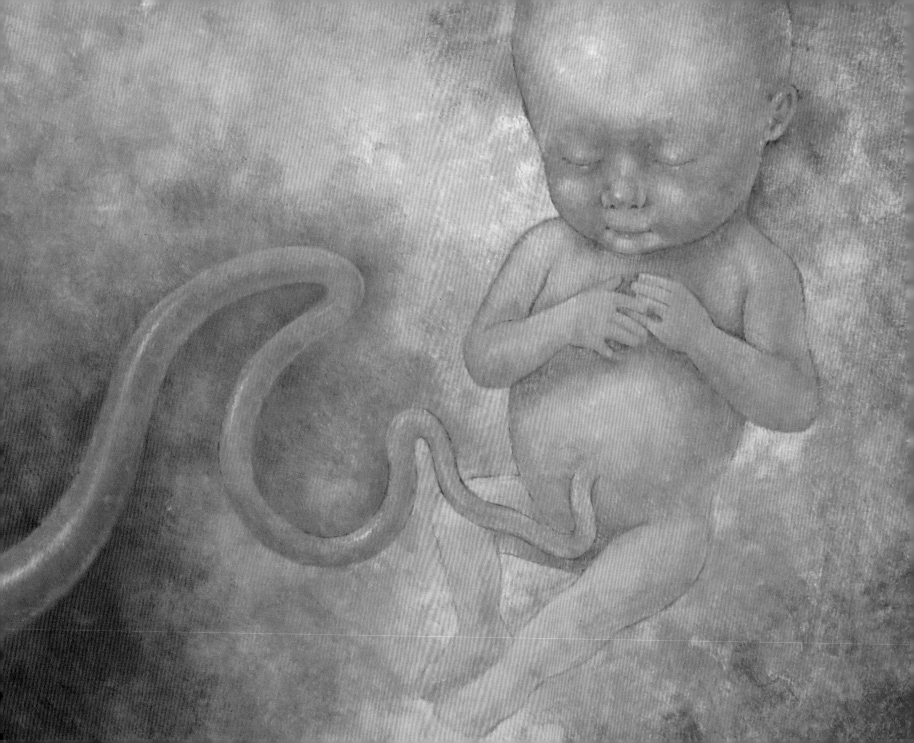

WEEK 13

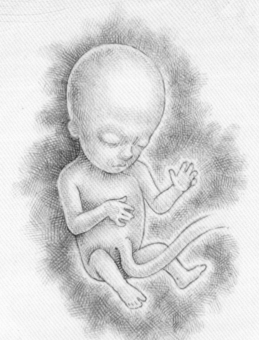

And precious is their blood in his sight.

— Psalm 72:14

I am beginning to grow much more rapidly now. Although I only weigh about half an ounce, I'm roughly the size of a peach and twice as long as I was a month ago. I'd like to report another new development: Up until now, Mom's blood has always helped to feed me, protect me, and get rid of anything I don't need. I'm proud to say that my own blood supply is now able to help with this important task. Hurrah!

WEEK 14

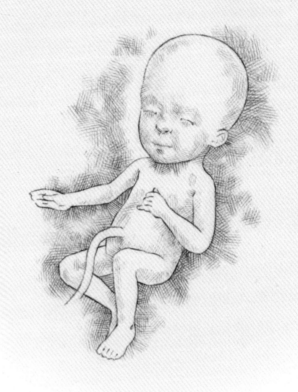

And they said to him, "Do you hear what these are saying?" And Jesus said to them, "Yes; have you never read,
'Out of the mouths of babies and infants you have brought perfect praise'?"

— Matthew 21:16

If you could see me now, you would know whether I am a boy or a girl. Also, my vocal cords are starting to form for the day when I will sing Christmas carols with Mom and Dad during this joyful season. Another bit of news is that I can grasp and hold things, thanks to my amazing thumbs. Before you know it, I will use them to open Christmas presents under the tree.

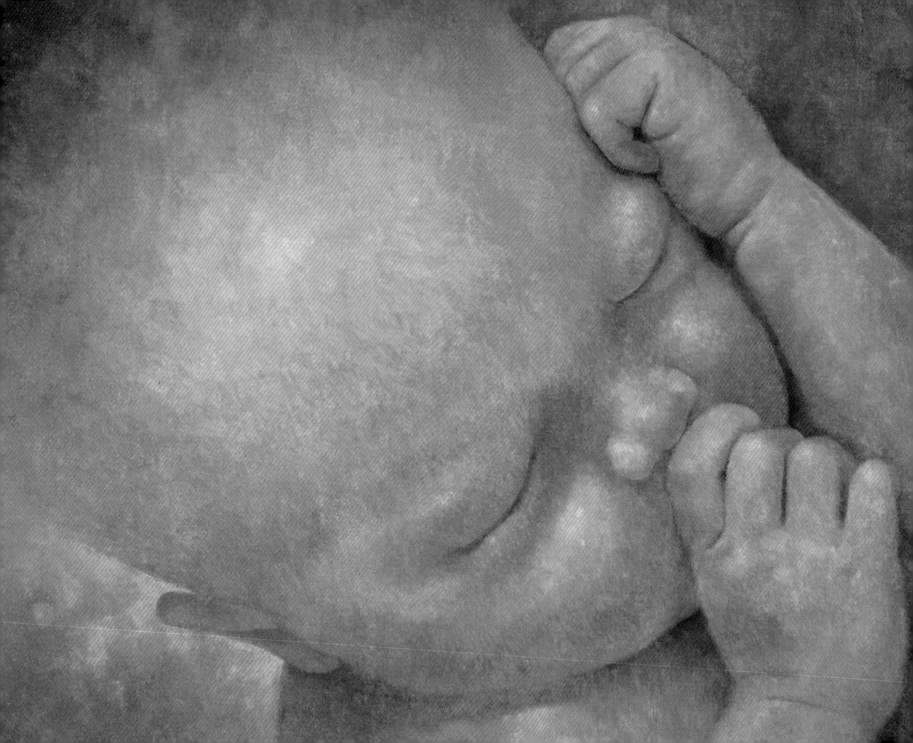

WEEK 15

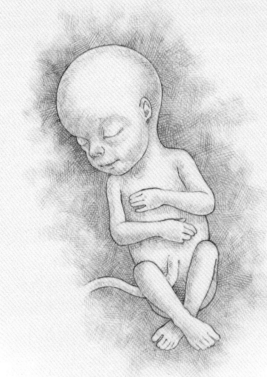

"In him we live and move and have our being";
as even some of your poets have said,
"For we are indeed his offspring."

— Acts of the Apostles 17:28

I've had a real growth spurt! I'm about the size of a large orange. My thumb finds its way to my mouth more and more now. Perhaps I may continue with this habit after I'm born, depending on my unique personality. Another one of God's amazing secrets is that already some of my movements, as well as my temperament, are similar to Mom's and Dad's even though I won't see them for another five months. Merry Christmas, family!

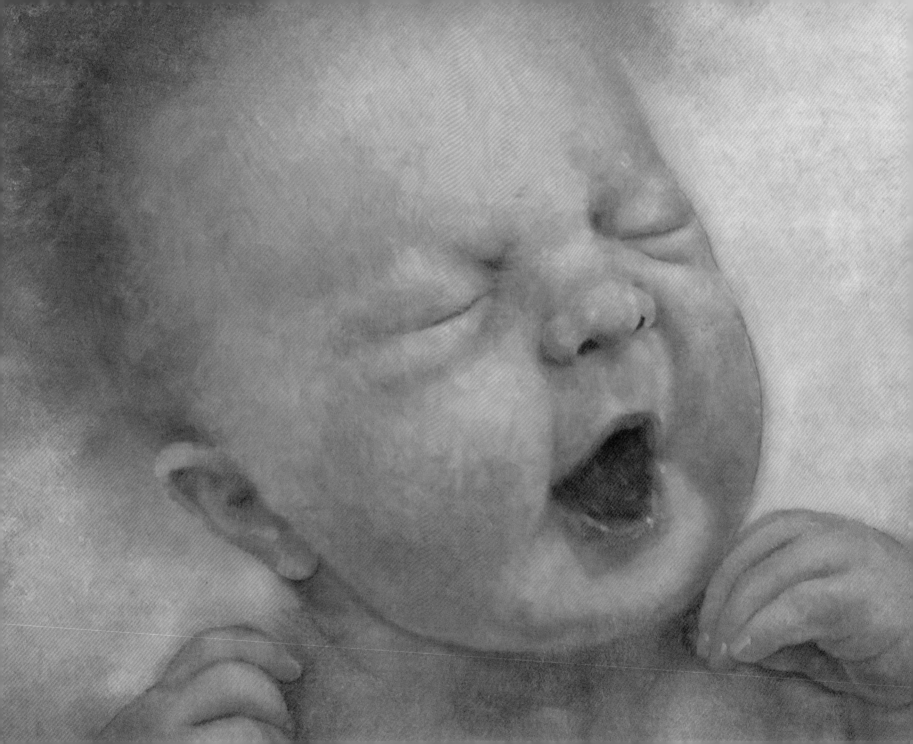

WEEK 16

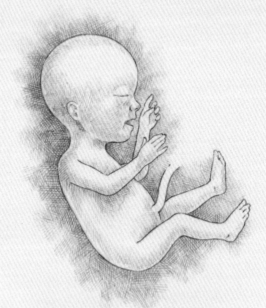

A glad heart makes a cheerful countenance.

— *Proverbs 15:13*

I can hold my head straight now and practice some of my new facial expressions. You might think I'm acting a bit like a clown as I grimace, squint, blink, and smile. Newly formed eyebrows and eyelashes add sparkle to the faces I make. A closer look with an X-ray would show a clear picture of my wonderful and amazing bones, which are now knit together and becoming hardened.

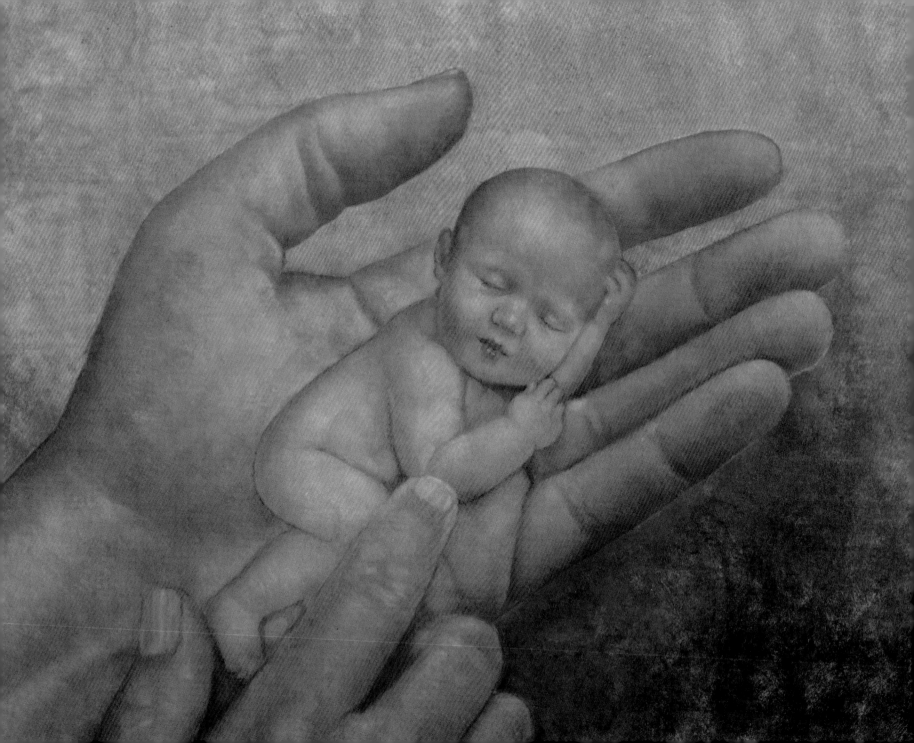

WEEK 17

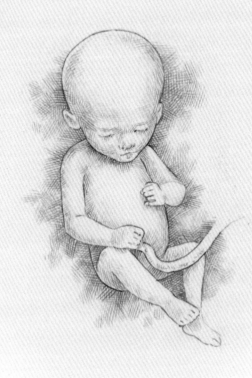

Can a woman forget her sucking child,
*   that she should have no compassion on the*
*   son of her womb?*
Even these may forget,
*   yet I will not forget you.*

— Isaiah 49:15

Today I weigh almost five ounces and could fit in the palm of my mother's hand. I am starting to get a special kind of baby fat, called "brown fat," which will help keep me warm throughout my whole life. Another important piece of news: I can now breathe underwater. Drawing the fluid in and out helps to strengthen and develop my lungs. Isn't God a genius?

WEEK 18

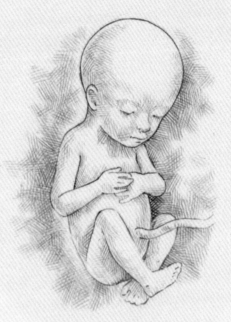

Let your father and mother be glad,
let her who bore you rejoice.

— *Proverbs 23:25*

Flutters and flips, here I am! Can you feel me now, Mom? I am finally big enough to say hello back to you! Everything in here is going according to God's plan.

WEEK 19

And the peace of God, which passes all understanding, will keep your hearts and your minds in Christ Jesus.

— Philippians 4:7

If you measured me in a sitting position (from my bottom to the top of my head), I'd be about the size of a large sweet potato. My body is quickly growing, so my head no longer appears to be much bigger than the rest of me. My brain is developing in leaps and bounds; every sixty seconds, 100,000 new brain cells are forming. This new "telegraph" system helps me plan my movements.

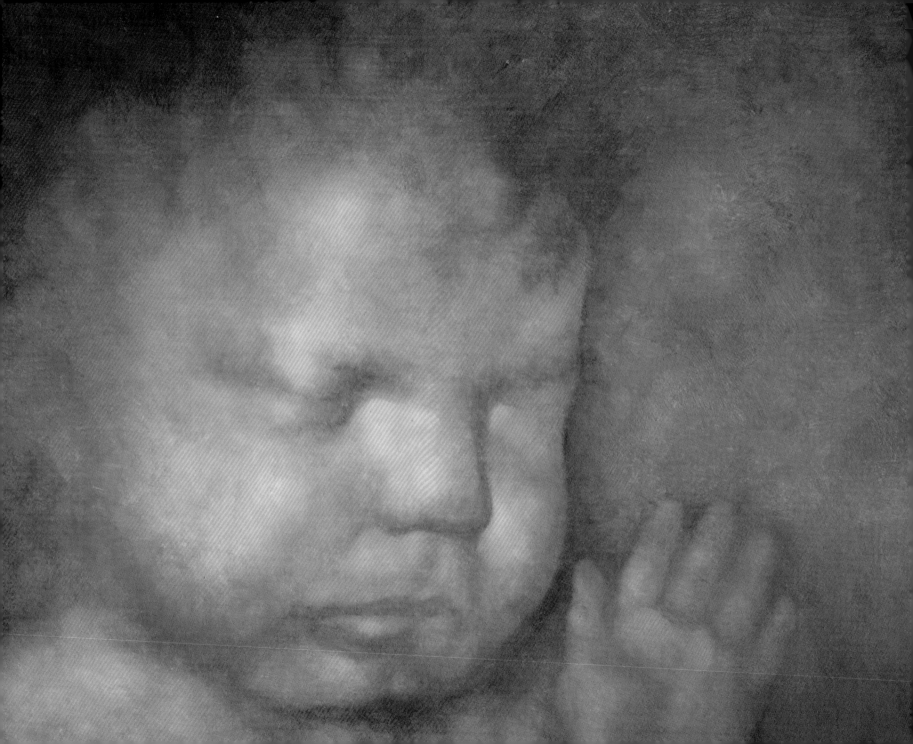

WEEK 20

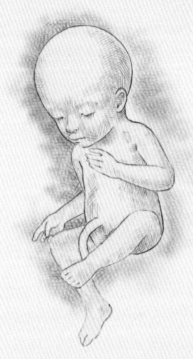

So God created man in his own image,
in the image of God he created him;
male and female he created them.

— Genesis 1:27

We had an ultrasound this week, and my parents saw what Mom already knew: where I like to lay my head and place my hands and feet. They got to see some of the things I can do, like opening and closing my fingers. Dad said that I was waving to them. This is the time the technician could have revealed whether I am a boy or a girl. I wonder … did they choose to know now or save it for a surprise on my birthday?

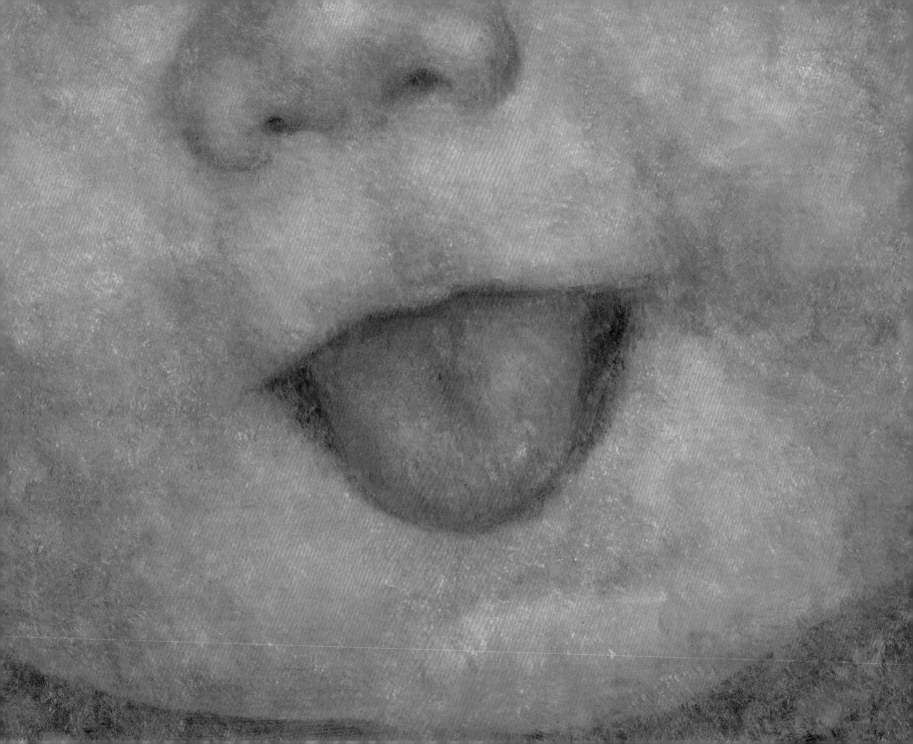

WEEK 21

*O taste and see that the L*ORD *is good!*
Blessed is the man who takes refuge
in him!

— Psalm 34:8

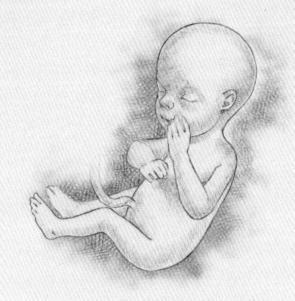

This week it is all about my tongue, which is fully developed now. My new favorite thing to do is to practice swallowing and moving my tongue in and out. My taste buds are working well, and I can even tell what Mom likes to eat best. When she eats something with a strong taste, it makes me scowl. All this helps me to get ready for the glorious day when I taste my first milk. Over halfway to my birthday now!

WEEK 22

*I can do all things in him
who strengthens me.*

— Philippians 4:13

I am about the size of a small eggplant and weigh almost as much. My mother sure can feel me moving these days, as my legs and arms are gaining more and more strength. My activities fall into a pattern of sorts; I like to exercise, rest, explore, rest some more, then begin all over again. I am also adjusting to Mom's daily schedule, and as our bodies become more and more in rhythm with each other, so do our hearts. Happy Valentine's Day, Mom!

WEEK 23

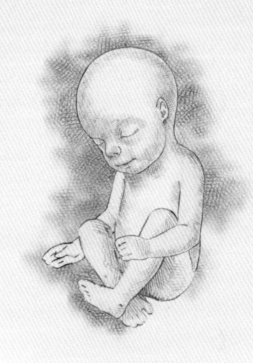

But, as it is written,
   "What no eye has seen, nor ear heard,
   nor the heart of man conceived,
   what God has prepared for those who
      love him."

— *1 Corinthians 2:9*

I weigh about one whole pound now. I am not growing quite as fast as I was before, since certain parts of me are becoming more refined. Take my eyes, for instance: they are fully formed except for their color, which has yet to be revealed. I wonder … will they be the same color as Mom's or Dad's, or one of my ancestors? Only God knows right now.

WEEK 24

Sacrifice and offering you do not desire;
  but you have given me an open ear. Burnt
offering and sin offering you
  have not required.
Then I said, "Behold, I come;
  in the roll of the book it is written of me;
I delight to do your will, O my God;
  your law is within my heart."

— *Psalm 40:6–8*

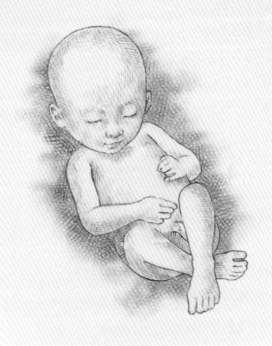

Would you believe that I look almost exactly as I will at birth, only a lot smaller? My little world is really expanding and becoming more exciting, because now I can hear sounds from the outside. Today I heard music and a dog barking. Last night I could hear Dad's deep voice when he was reading to Mom. This gift of hearing truly helps me begin to connect with God's creation. He thought of everything!

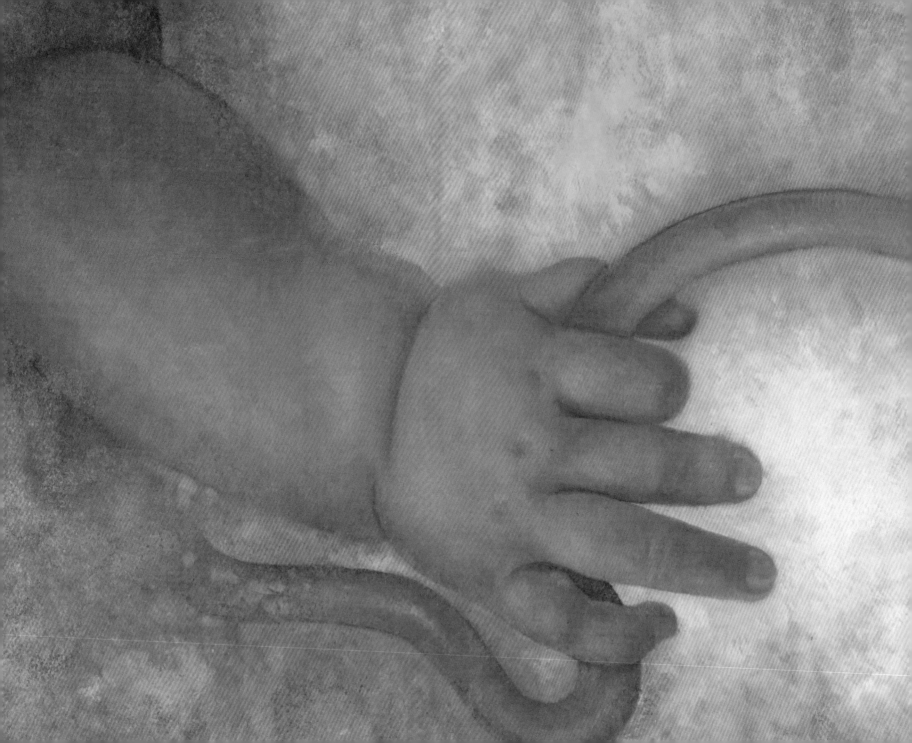

WEEK 25

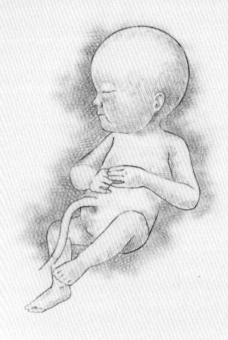

For I, the Lord your God,
*   hold your right hand;*
it is I who say to you, "Fear not,
*   I will help you."*

— *Isaiah 41:13*

I am the size of a small butternut squash, roughly nine inches from head to bottom, and I weigh about a pound and a half. Touch was one of my first senses to mature. I'm having fun with these awesome hands of mine, exploring my face and body and feeling the walls that surround me. I can even make a fist and can grasp my umbilical cord — my lifeline to my mother.

WEEK 26

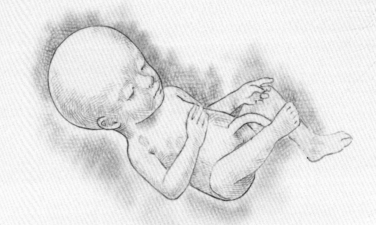

Open my eyes, that I may behold
wondrous things out of your law.

— *Psalm 119:18*

Glorious day! My eyes are fully opened. They had been sealed shut for several weeks as they were under construction. At last I can rehearse my blinking skills when I'm awake, and if I'm ready for a nap, I can close them just like Mom and Dad. My brain is growing at lightning speed.

WEEK 27

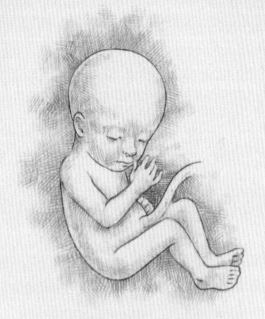

*And I will lay sinews upon you, and will cause flesh to come upon you, and cover you with skin, and put breath in you, and you shall live; and you shall know that I am the L*ORD.

— Ezekiel 37:6

Right now, if I were measured from head to toe, I would be around fifteen inches long. If you could see my skin now, you would think it's a little wrinkled and hangs a bit loose. That's just because it's waiting for the fat to catch up. It has a rosy color because that's what happens first before it gets its very own skin tone. It is getting thicker and thicker, and oh, it's going to be so beautiful!

WEEK 28

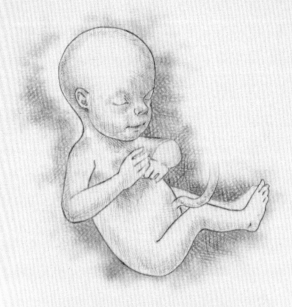

For God speaks in one way,
and in two, though man does not
perceive it.
In a dream, in a vision of the night,
when deep sleep falls upon men,
while they slumber on their beds.

— Job 33:14—15

Can you believe that I weigh about two pounds and am about fifteen and a half inches long? Now that I am so big, I have been working on many new movements, like stretching and coughing. But a really exciting new thing for me is that I am beginning to have dreams. My favorite dream is the one where I see my parents.

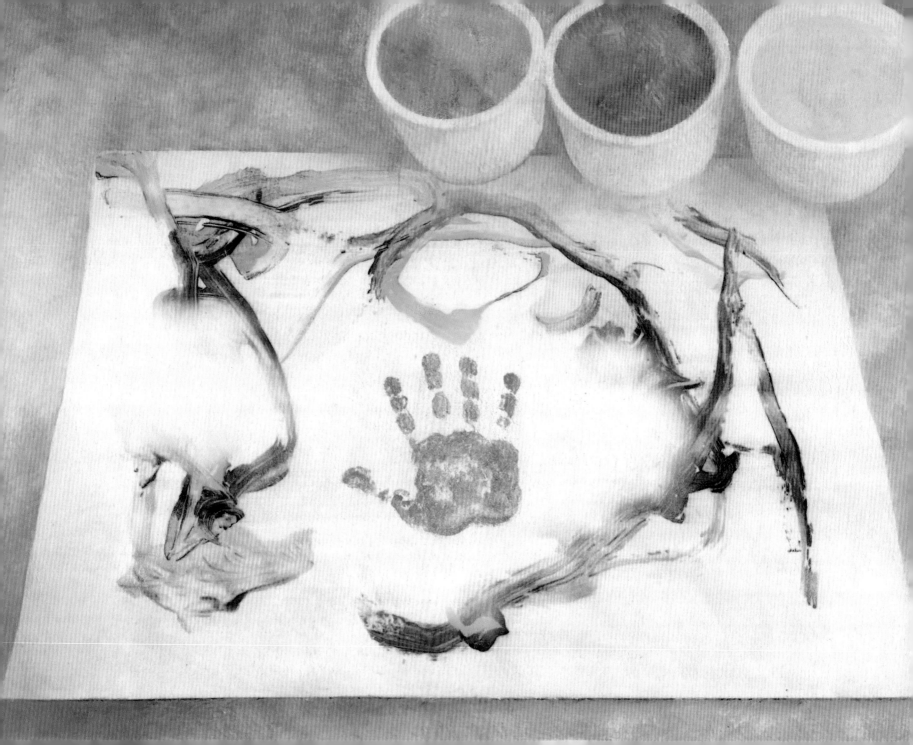

WEEK 29

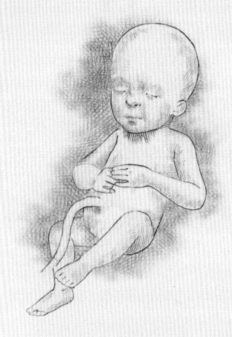

*Your hands have made and fashioned me;
give me understanding that I may learn
your commandments.*

— *Psalm 119:73*

Mom and Dad went to the doctor again today, and they could hear my heartbeat using an ordinary stethoscope. My parents were so excited! Another new development is that creases are starting to develop on my fingers. Soon I will have my very own unique fingerprints. God is so creative!

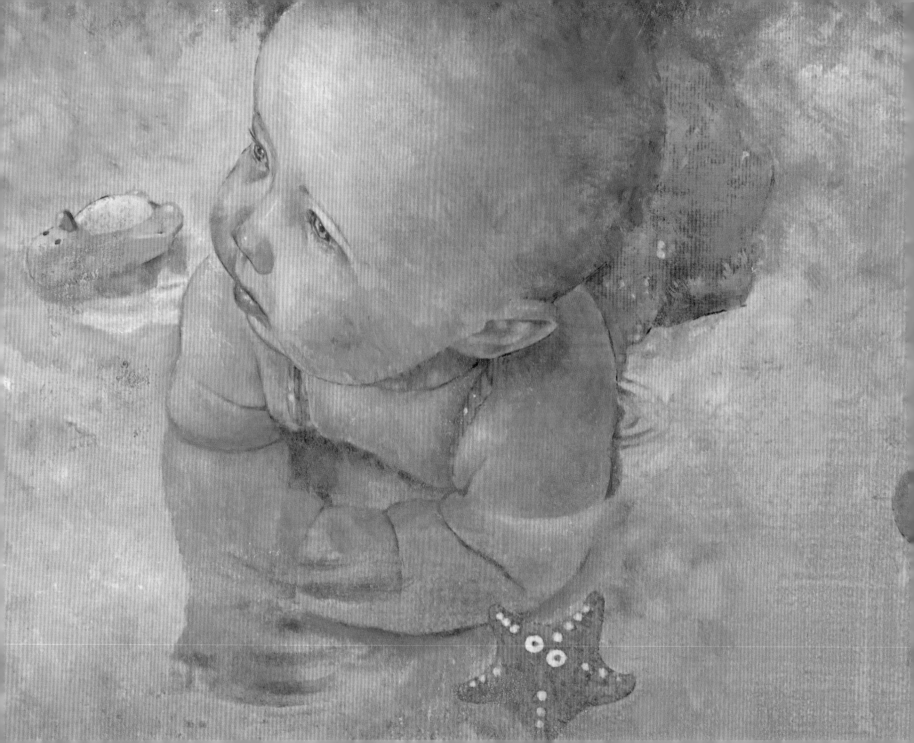

WEEK 30

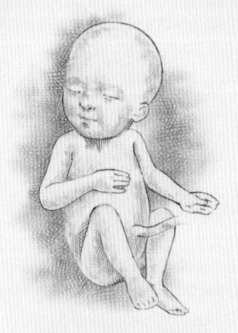

The spirit of God has made me,
*   and the breath of the Almighty*
*   gives me life.*

— *Job 33:4*

I weigh almost three pounds and am about sixteen and a half inches long. Although I am so big that it's getting pretty cramped in here, there are still many things for me to work on. For instance, I am becoming an expert in my underwater breathing exercises. All of this prepares me for the day when I will breathe only air, just like Mom and Dad. Who knows? Maybe I'll even be on the swim team when I am older!

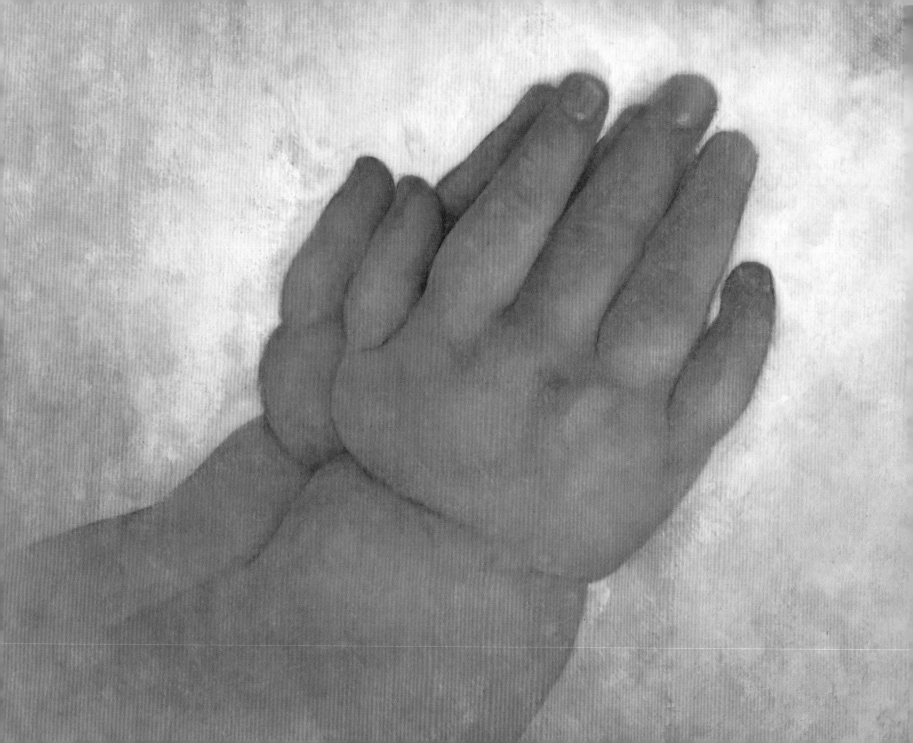

WEEK 31

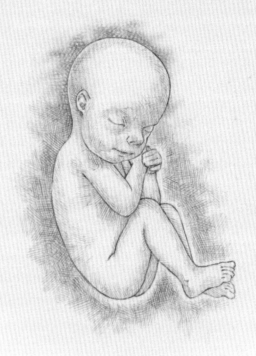

For I know the plans I have for you, says the Lord, plans for welfare and not for evil, to give you a future and a hope. Then you will call upon me and come and pray to me, and I will hear you. You will seek me and find me; when you seek me with all your heart, I will be found by you, says the Lord.

— *Jeremiah 29:11–14*

I grew another inch this week and weigh well over three pounds. If I were to be born now, I would look a lot like any newborn baby, only smaller. All my senses are working, and my chances of survival would be very good. Still, I think it's probably best if I camp out here for a while longer.

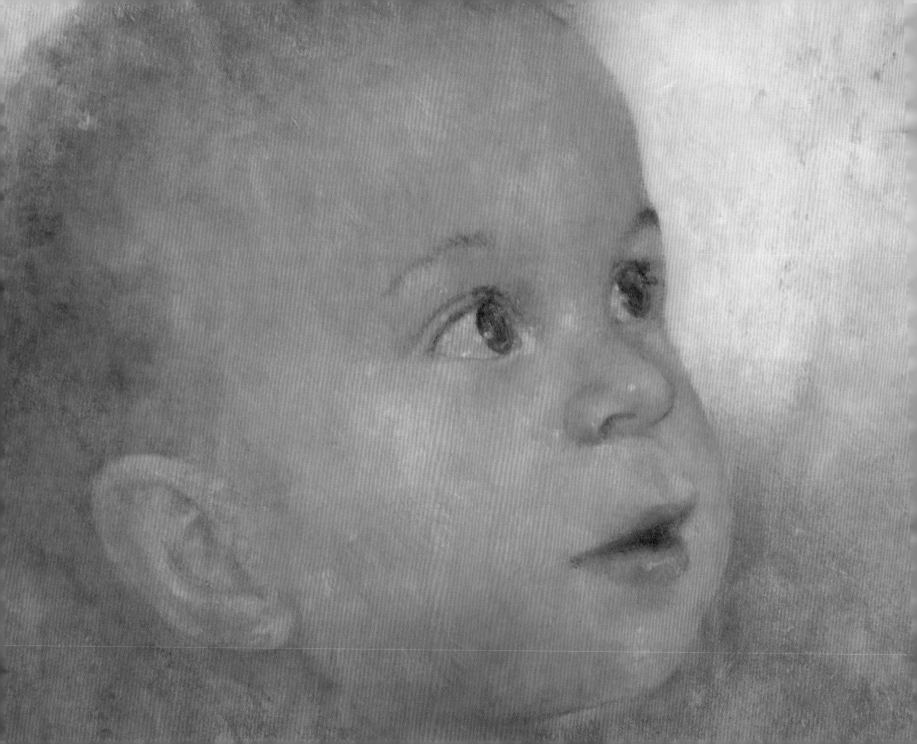

WEEK 32

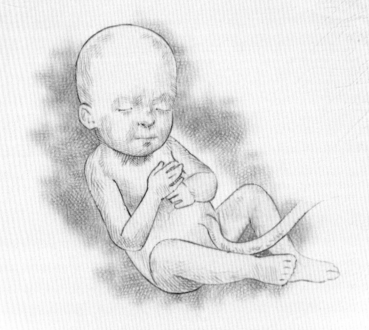

To him the gatekeeper opens; the sheep hear his voice, and he calls his own sheep by name and leads them out. When he has brought out all his own, he goes before them, and the sheep follow him, for they know his voice.

— John 10:3–4

My sense of hearing is my main connection with the outside world. As I continue to grow day by day, I am able to hear more and more new sounds. God has made my ears to be especially attuned to a woman's voice. I love it when you sing and talk to me, Mom. And you know what? I will already recognize your voice as soon as I am born.

WEEK 33

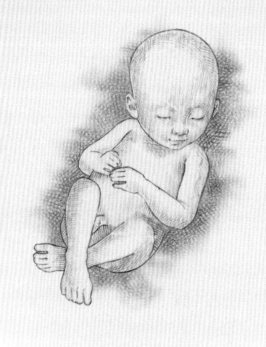

And when Elizabeth heard the greeting of Mary, the child leaped in her womb; and Elizabeth was filled with the Holy Spirit and she exclaimed with a loud cry, "Blessed are you among women, and blessed is the fruit of your womb! And why is this granted me, that the mother of my Lord should come to me? For behold, when the voice of your greeting came to my ears, the child in my womb leaped for joy."

— Luke 1:41–44

I am about four and a half pounds and over nineteen inches long. It's getting more crowded than ever in here! Looks like my water ballet days are over … but I can still give Mom a good poke with my hand or a jab with my foot. I made my last turn today, and I'm in my birth position. Our big day will be here before you know it.

WEEK 34

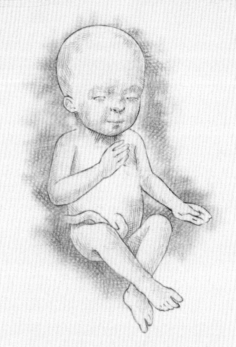

For he satisfies him who is thirsty,
  and the hungry he fills with good things.

— Psalm 107:9

Wow! I have more taste buds now than I will at any other time in my life. I can even tell which foods you like best, Mom, and I'm sure glad you like ice cream. I wonder what my favorite flavor will be. I can't wait to see what kind we'll have together this time next year. Happy Mother's Day, Mom!

WEEK 35

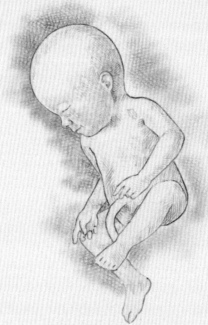

*O that you would kiss me with
the kisses of your mouth!*

— Song of Solomon 1:2

I weigh a little over five pounds; that's more than a whole bag of sugar! I'm really becoming plump now. My wrinkles are disappearing, and my skin is getting softer and smoother. This is how God designs sweet baby skin that Mom and Dad will love to touch, kiss, and smell.

WEEK 36

Are not five sparrows sold for two pennies?
And not one of them is forgotten before
God. Why, even the hairs of your head
are all numbered. Fear not; you are of
more value than many sparrows.

— Luke 12:6–7

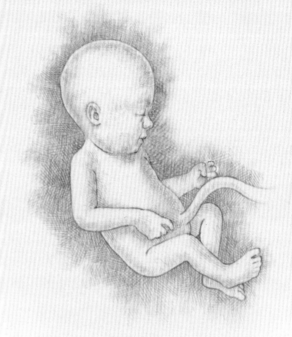

All my systems are nearly ready to go now, except for my lungs, which continue to be "under construction." This is really important, because I will need them to work on their own once I am born. I am also growing more and more hair on my head. I can't tell what color it is, but it sure is interesting to grab with my fingers.

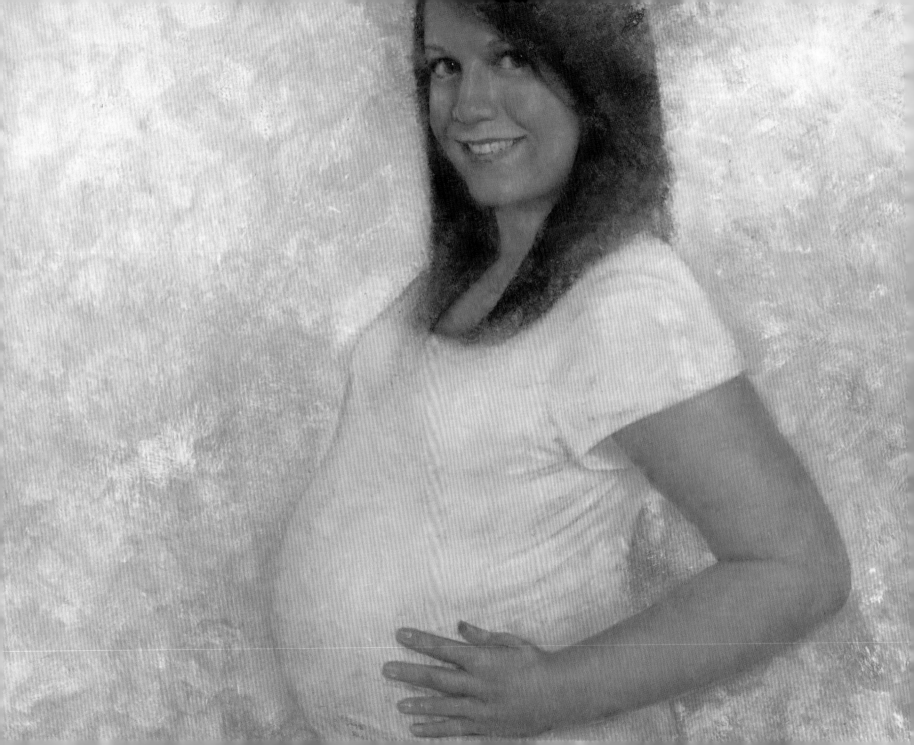

WEEK 37

O Lord, you have searched me and
    known me!
You know when I sit down and when
    I rise up;
    you discern my thoughts from afar.
You search out my path and my lying down,
    and are acquainted with all my ways.

— Psalm 139:1–3

My little world in here is getting brighter all the time, since I am stretching Mom's belly more and more. My eyes can see much better, and I love to turn toward the light and play. It's fun to see what I can do with my fingers and toes. When it gets dark, I like to sleep, just like Mom does. I am practicing what my parents call a "daily routine." How am I doing?

WEEK 38

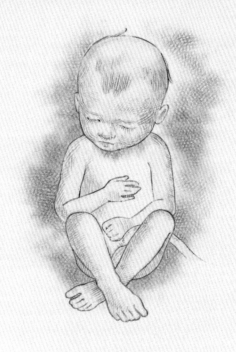

The Lord called me from the womb,
from the body of my mother he named
my name.
He made my mouth like a sharp sword,
in the shadow of his hand he hid me;
he made me a polished arrow,
in his quiver he hid me away.

— Isaiah 49:1–2

Can you believe that I weigh almost seven pounds now? These days one of my jobs is to add more fat, and I am gaining more than half an ounce per day. My next big job is to become a pro at breathing. Sometimes the water gets into my windpipe and gives me a strong case of the hiccups. When this happens, I can hear Mom chuckle. I guess it makes her belly jump! Do you think that's why she calls me her Little Jumping Bean?

WEEK 39

How precious is your mercy, O God!
The children of men take refuge in
the shadow of your wings.

— *Psalm 36:7*

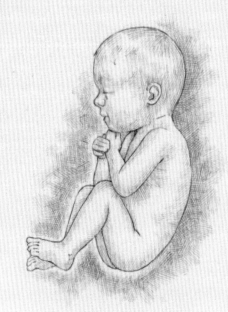

I am spending quite a bit of time sleeping as I get ready for my big day. It won't be long now … When I am awake, I like listening to all kinds of sounds and feeling my very, very tight surroundings. (And I thought things were snug a few weeks ago!) I am still adding on fat to keep me warm. It's building up around my neck, shoulders, and other important places in my body. This is another way God protects me, since I can't shiver yet or ask for a "blankie."

WEEK 40

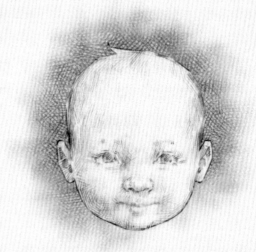

Whoever receives one such child in my name receives me; and whoever receives me, receives not me but him who sent me.

— *Mark 9:37*

Today is the big day! It sure was a hard and exhausting trip, but it was well worth it. I am now snuggling on Mom's chest, feeling safe and warm with the one whose scent I have known since I could first smell. Now I get to hear her voice and heartbeat and even feel her breath from the outside. We are filled with so much love as we gaze into each other's eyes for the very first time.

I am in for another treat as she presents me to Dad and our eyes lock together. Wow! I know your voice too, Dad, from all those times you talked to me. Bet you didn't think I was listening!

I can feel God loving each one of us just as I have felt him loving me from the very beginning. I can't wait to begin the many adventures that our family will share together.

Happy Father's Day, Dad!

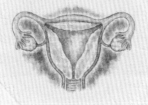

Week 1

Week 2

Week 3

Week 4

Week 5

Week 11

Week 12

Week 13

Week 14

Week 15

Not to scale

Week 6

Week 7

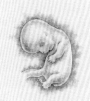

Week 8

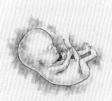

Week 9

Week 10

Week 16

Week 17

Week 18

Week 19

Week 20

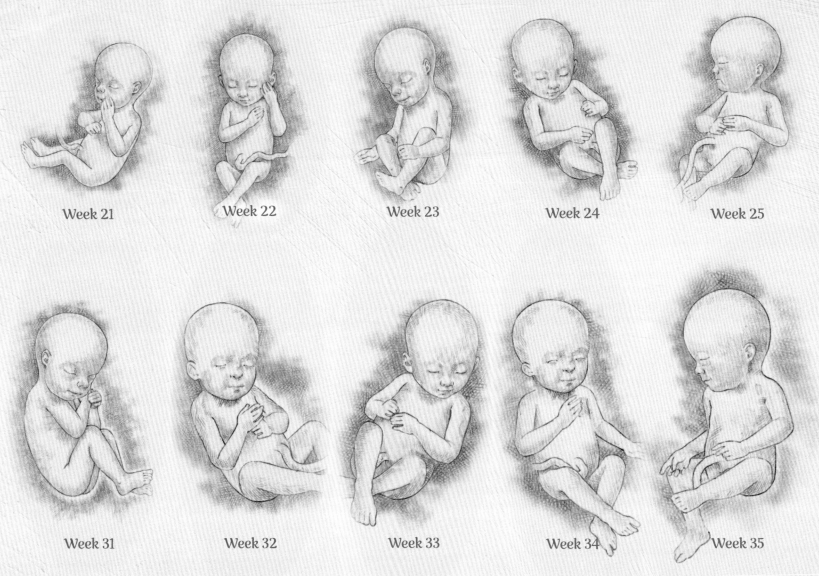

Week 21   Week 22   Week 23   Week 24   Week 25

Week 31   Week 32   Week 33   Week 34   Week 35

Not to scale

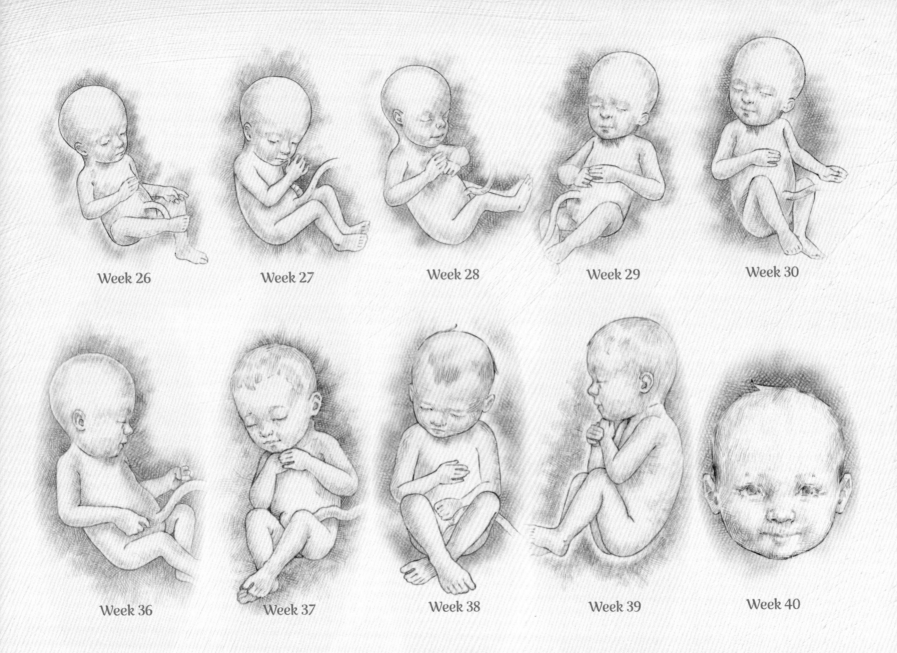

Week 26   Week 27   Week 28   Week 29   Week 30

Week 36   Week 37   Week 38   Week 39   Week 40

BIBLIOGRAPHY

Curtis, Glade B. *Your Pregnancy Week by Week*. New York: Perseus, 2000.

Dihle, Vicki L., and Beck, Bradley G. *The First 9 Months*. Colorado Springs, CO: Focus on the Family, 1999.

MacDougall, Jane. *Pregnancy Week-by-Week*. New York: Harper, 1997.

My Secret Life. Stafford, VA: American Life League, 2005.

Nilsson, Lennart. *A Child Is Born*. New York: Delacorte Press, 1965.

"Stages of Pregnancy Week by Week." Parents.com. http://www.parents.com/pregnancy/week-by-week/.

Tsiaras, Alexander. *From Conception to Birth: A Life Unfolds*. New York: Doubleday, 2002.

ABOUT THE AUTHORS

REV. BILL DESCHAMPS

After twenty years of military service, Bill was called to the priesthood. Ordained in 1990, his love for God continues to grow daily. As pastor of St. Patrick's in Jaffrey and Sacred Heart in Greenville, New Hampshire, he noticed a decline of children in the community and felt the need to write a book that would promote life from the moment of conception.

CHRISTINE SCHROEDER

Christine worked with individuals with special needs most of her life, spending several years as a childbirth educator and assistant midwife. She is passionate about the worth of every human being, especially the young or otherwise vulnerable.

MARY ROMA

Mary is a retired New York State teacher. She enjoyed teaching the early primary grades. Mary is the mother of a stillborn baby boy. She now resides with her husband, Al, in southwestern New Hampshire.

SUSAN JOY BELLAVANCE

Susan Joy Bellavance served with the Missionaries of Charity, later becoming a parochial school teacher and a founding member of Mount Royal Academy, Sunapee, New Hampshire. She is currently a Catholic children's author. Susan's books include *King of the Shattered Glass*, *Will You Come to Mass?*, and *The Light of Christmas Morning*.

ABOUT THE ILLUSTRATOR

DAN ANDREASEN

Dan has created artwork for more than fifty picture books. He has also written and illustrated seven others with a style that has been described by Kirkus as "cunning and clever." He is the author and illustrator of *The Giant of Seville*, which School Library Journal called in a starred review "a standout package." Dan is the illustrator of two of the American Girl historical characters: Felicity and Samantha. His publishing clients include Harper Collins, Simon and Schuster, Scholastic, Abrams, Disney-Hyperion, Henry Holt, Random House, American Girl, and Holiday House. Dan's graphic designs have been used to advertise a wide variety of products including Oscar Meyer, Chef Boyardee, Folgers, Harley-Davidson, Orville Redenbacher, Kraft, and Marks and Spencer. He lives with his family in Medina, Ohio.